KANSAS CITY
ROYALS

by Paul Bowker

SportsZone

An Imprint of Abdo Publishing
www.abdopublishing.com

www.abdopublishing.com

Published by Abdo Publishing, a division of ABDO, PO Box 398166, Minneapolis, Minnesota 55439. Copyright © 2015 by Abdo Consulting Group, Inc. International copyrights reserved in all countries. No part of this book may be reproduced in any form without written permission from the publisher. SportsZone™ is a trademark and logo of Abdo Publishing.

Printed in the United States of America, North Mankato, Minnesota
052014
092014

THIS BOOK CONTAINS
RECYCLED MATERIALS

Editor: Matt Tustison
Copy Editor: Nicholas Cafarelli
Interior Design and Production: Christa Schneider
Cover Design: Christa Schneider

Photo Credits: G. Newman Lowrance/AP Images, cover; Eric Gay/AP Images, title; Cliff Schiappa, File/AP Images, 4, 42 (bottom); AP Images, 6, 16, 23, 24, 27, 30, 42 (middle), 44; The Kansas City Star, Patrick Sullivan/AP Images, 8; Photo by Focus on Sport/Getty Images, 11; Photo by: Diamond Images/Getty Images, 12, 42 (top); Photo by: John Vawter Collection/Diamond Images/Getty Images, 15, 19; Richard Drew/AP Images, 21; Photo by Bruce Bennett Studios/Getty Images, 28; Chris Corsmeier/AP Images, 32; Kevork Djansezian/AP Images, 35, 43 (top); Phil Long/AP Images, 37; Ed Zurga/AP Images, 38, 43 (middle); Charlie Riedel/AP Images, 41, 43 (bottom); Reed Hoffmann/AP Images, 47

Library of Congress Control Number: 2014933081
Cataloging-in-Publication Data
Bowker, Paul, 1954-
  Kansas City Royals / by Paul Bowker.
    p. cm. — (Inside MLB)
  Includes bibliographical references and index.
  ISBN 978-1-62403-472-5
  1. Kansas City Royals (Baseball team)—History—Juvenile literature. I. Title.
  GV875.K3B69 2015
  796.357'6409778411—dc23
                    2014933081

TABLE OF CONTENTS

CHAPTER 1

WORLD SERIES CHAMPS

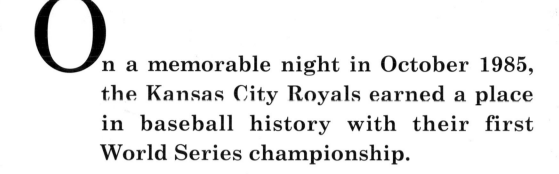

O

n a memorable night in October 1985, the Kansas City Royals earned a place in baseball history with their first World Series championship.

On October 27, 1985, the Royals routed the St. Louis Cardinals 11–0 in Game 7 of a World Series that was dubbed the "I-70 Series." The I-70 highway runs through Kansas City, located in western Missouri on the Missouri-Kansas border, and St. Louis, located in eastern Missouri on the Missouri-Illinois border.

I-70 World Series

Kansas City and St. Louis are located 249 miles (400 km) apart along Interstate 70 in Missouri. The 1985 World Series between the Royals and the Cardinals was thus known as the "I-70 Series." It also was called the "Show-Me Series" because Missouri is known as the "Show-Me State." After the Series was over, Royals star third baseman George Brett said of the Cardinals, "We showed 'em."

Third baseman George Brett, *left*, and pitcher Bret Saberhagen celebrate after the Royals beat the Cardinals 11–0 in Game 7 of the 1985 World Series.

Kansas City players, including George Brett, *front*, are a happy bunch on October 27, 1985, after the Royals won the World Series.

A large celebration got underway at Royals Stadium. The World Series title was the first for the Royals. They became the fifth team to win the best-of-seven Series after trailing three games to one.

Bret Saberhagen, the Most Valuable Player (MVP) of the Series, pitched a shutout in Game 7. He allowed just five hits. Third baseman George Brett, catcher Jim Sundberg, and other Royals mobbed Saberhagen after Darryl Motley caught the game-ending fly ball in right field. Soon, Kansas City players were pouring champagne over each other in the clubhouse.

"We won the World Series, even if people said we weren't from a big enough city in the world to do it," Brett said.

Because the turf at that time at Royals Stadium was artificial, fans could not grab a piece of grass to keep as a souvenir. Instead, they jumped onto the field and threw dirt into the air. Kansas Citians watching the game on television left their homes to run into the streets in celebration. Motorists drove down the avenues honking horns.

Game 7 was certainly worth celebrating for the Royals and their fans. Kansas City was ahead 5–0 after four innings. That was thanks, in part, to a two-run home run by Motley in the second inning off John Tudor. The Royals broke the game open with six runs in the fifth inning. St. Louis manager Whitey Herzog and pitcher

Joaquin Andujar were ejected during that inning for arguing with home-plate umpire Don Denkinger over balls and strikes. Denkinger had made a controversial call the night before in the ninth inning of Game 6. With Game 7 getting out of hand, the Cardinals took out their frustration on him.

Motley finished with three hits and three runs batted in (RBIs) in Game 7. Brett went 4-for-5 and scored two runs. Leadoff man Lonnie Smith had

Comeback Kids

The 1985 Royals became the fifth team in major league history to win the World Series after trailing the best-of-seven series three games to one. The previous four teams to accomplish the feat were the 1925 Pittsburgh Pirates (against the Washington Senators), the 1958 New York Yankees (against the Milwaukee Braves), the 1968 Detroit Tigers (against the St. Louis Cardinals), and the 1979 Pirates (against the Baltimore Orioles).

Cardinals pitcher Todd Worrell catches the ball at first base, but umpire Don Denkinger would rule the Royals' Jorge Orta safe on a controversial call in Game 6 of the 1985 World Series.

two RBIs and scored two runs. The Royals won the Series' final two games at their home ball-park, Royals Stadium.

Kansas City had prevailed 2–1 in Game 6 with the help of what became known as "The Call" in the bottom of the ninth inning. Denkinger was the first-base umpire in that game.

With the Royals trailing 1–0, Denkinger ruled leadoff batter Jorge Orta safe at first on a close play. Orta hit a grounder to first baseman Jack Clark, who tossed the ball to pitcher Todd Worrell. Replays indicated that Worrell caught the throw from Clark in time for the out. But Denkinger ruled Orta safe.

Steve Balboni followed with a single, putting runners at first and second. Sundberg attempted a sacrifice bunt. But Worrell threw to third for a force-out. St. Louis catcher Darrell Porter's passed ball allowed the runners to move up to second and third. St. Louis intentionally walked pinch-hitter Hal McRae to load the bases. With the bases filled and one out, pinch-hitter Dane Iorg blooped a single to right field. Pinch-runner Onix Concepcion scored the tying run. Sundberg slid in with the winning run, just beating an on-target throw from Andy Van Slyke.

The Royals were ecstatic. Iorg suffered a broken nose in the celebration when he was swarmed by teammates. The Cardinals returned to their clubhouse dejected. After the game, Peter Ueberroth, commissioner of Major League Baseball (MLB), informed Denkinger that he had made an incorrect call.

The Royals' 1985 postseason ride featured plenty of drama in the American League Championship Series (ALCS) against the Toronto Blue Jays as well. Kansas City also had to overcome a three-games-to-one deficit in that series. The Royals won the final two games at Exhibition Stadium in Toronto. Kansas City prevailed 6–2 in

Big Year for Brett

Star third baseman George Brett had been to the playoffs six times with Kansas City before 1985, but it was not until his seventh trip to the postseason that he and the Royals won it all. Brett batted .335 with 30 home runs and 112 RBIs in the 1985 regular season, finishing second in the AL MVP voting. Brett also won the only Gold Glove Award of his career. In the ALCS against Toronto, Brett was named MVP. He hit three homers, including two in Game 3. He then batted .370 in the World Series.

BRET SABERHAGEN

The Royals' Bret Saberhagen was named the MVP of the 1985 World Series. The young right-hander was the winning pitcher in Games 3 and 7, throwing complete games both times. He allowed one run and six hits in Game 3, which Kansas City won 6–1, and then pitched a five-hit shutout in the Royals' 11–0 victory in Game 7.

Saberhagen also gained a son during the Series—the morning of the same day Game 6 was played. On October 26, Saberhagen's wife, Janeane, gave birth to the couple's first child, Drew William Saberhagen.

Saberhagen was inconsistent on the mound after his 1985 success. But he could be dominant. He went 23–6 in 1989, when he won a second Cy Young Award. The Royals traded Saberhagen to the New York Mets after the 1991 season. He retired after pitching for the Boston Red Sox in 2001.

Game 7. Saberhagen started for the Royals. But he lasted just three innings due to injury. Charlie Leibrandt allowed two runs in 5 1/3 innings of relief and earned the win. Brett was named the MVP of the ALCS. He batted .348 and slugged three home runs.

Everything fell into place for Kansas City in 1985. Saberhagen, just 21 years old, won the AL Cy Young Award, given to the league's top pitcher. The right-hander with pinpoint control finished 20–6 with a 2.87 earned-run average (ERA) in just his second big-league season. The Royals finished 91–71. They edged out the California Angels to win the AL West Division. Kansas City had fewer victories than baseball's other division winners that season—St. Louis (101), Toronto (99), and the Los

Bret Saberhagen pitches in the 1985 World Series. In his two World Series starts that year, Saberhagen went 2–0 with an ERA of 0.50.

Angeles Dodgers (95). But the Royals were good enough to make the playoffs. Once they were there, they made the most of their opportunity.

The 1985 title is the crowning achievement in the Royals' history. It also capped a glorious era in which the team made the playoffs seven times in a 10-year span. The last trip finally resulted in a coveted championship for Kansas City veterans such as Brett, McRae, and second baseman Frank White.

The Royals began playing in 1969 as an AL expansion franchise. Unlike most newcomers, they would not need very much time to start fielding highly competitive teams.

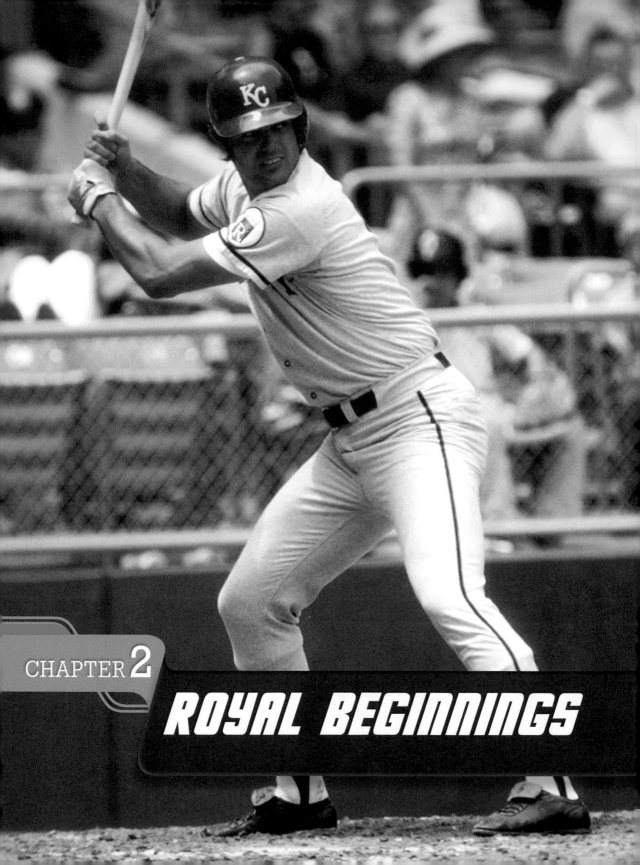

CHAPTER 2

ROYAL BEGINNINGS

The roots of the Royals can be traced to October 1967. That month, Charlie Finley, owner of the Kansas City Athletics, said he was moving the team to Oakland, California. MLB owners promised Kansas City another team by 1971. But Kansas Citians were angered by Finley's move. Kansas City had a rich baseball history. This included serving as the Athletics' home since 1955.

Sensing a passion for baseball in Kansas City, MLB club owners decided to quickly get the city an expansion team. Kansas City went just one year without a major league club, in 1968. A year later, the Royals—named out of respect to the Kansas City Monarchs, a team in the Negro Leagues—were welcomed into their temporary ballpark, Municipal Stadium.

The Royals began play in 1969 in the AL along with another new team, the Seattle Pilots. The Montreal Expos and

Lou Piniella, shown in 1972, was one of the Royals' top players in the expansion team's first few seasons. The left fielder played for Kansas City from 1969 to 1973.

THE MONARCHS

Kansas City had several baseball teams in the late 1800s and early 1900s. One of those teams was the major league Cowboys.

Another well-known team in Kansas City began play in 1920. The Monarchs were charter members of the Negro National League. The Monarchs played in that league until 1931. The Monarchs won the first Negro League World Series in 1924. The Monarchs were an independent team from 1932 to 1936 and then played in the Negro American League from 1937 to 1961. They again became an independent team before disbanding in 1965.

Once the big leagues started signing African-American players, the Monarchs sent more to the majors than any Negro Leagues team. One of those players was Jackie Robinson, who broke the modern-day color barrier when the Brooklyn Dodgers signed him.

the San Diego Padres were new teams in the National League (NL). The AL and the NL reorganized. They became leagues with two divisions each. The Royals and the Pilots were put in the AL West. The Pilots would move just one year later and become the Milwaukee Brewers.

Kansas City and Seattle participated in an AL expansion draft before the 1969 season. The Royals had the first pick and selected pitcher Roger Nelson from the Baltimore Orioles. In all, Kansas City chose 30 players. The Royals' first manager was Joe Gordon. He had previously managed the Athletics in 1961 and, before that, the Cleveland Indians and the Detroit Tigers.

The Royals finished 69–93 in 1969. They could take comfort in the fact that they had

Royals manager Joe Gordon watches his team during spring training in March 1969 in Fort Myers, Florida. Gordon was manager for one season.

the best record of MLB's four new teams. One of Kansas City's best moves early in its history was the acquisition of left fielder Lou Piniella. Seattle selected Piniella from Cleveland in the AL expansion draft. The Pilots then traded Piniella to the Royals. Piniella won the AL Rookie of the Year Award in 1969 with Kansas City. He batted .282 with 11 homers and 68 RBIs. He was a standout for the Royals for four more seasons before he was traded to the New York Yankees.

Kansas City was smartly building its team. This would become even more apparent in the 1970s.

CHAPTER 3

THE '70S: BUILDING A WINNER

Kansas City was a baseball construction zone in the early 1970s. While steel-workers were busily putting together the city's new $70 million ballpark that would open in 1973, the Royals were assembling a roster of talented players. They would help Kansas City rise more quickly in the standings than any big-league expansion team had previously.

In 1971, in just their third season, the Royals finished 85–76 and in second place in the AL West. Kansas City did this with the help of wise draft picks and outstanding trades.

In addition to acquiring left fielder Lou Piniella before the 1969 season, the Royals picked up center fielder Amos Otis in a deal with the New York Mets prior to the 1970 season. Otis became a standout with Kansas City. He hit a career-high .301, drove in 79 runs, and had an AL-best 52 stolen bases

Royals second baseman Frank White leaps while making a throw in Game 2 of the 1977 ALCS against the Yankees. White began a long career with Kansas City in 1973.

QUICK ON THEIR FEET

Speed was a big reason the Royals became a successful team. Center fielder Amos Otis led the AL in steals in 1971 with 52, and he would swipe more than 30 bases in five different seasons in the 1970s. Shortstop Freddie Patek reached the 30-steal mark every season from 1971 to 1978, leading the AL with 53 in 1977. Second baseman Frank White stole 20 or more bases three times in the 1970s. In 1976, outfielder Willie Wilson made his debut with the Royals. In 1978, he had 46 steals. The next year, he led the AL with 83 steals, and he followed that up with a 79-steal season in 1980.

Kansas City also displayed its speed by leading the AL in triples eight consecutive seasons, from 1975 to 1982. Kansas City ran wild on Royals Stadium's artificial turf, bunting and stealing on the surface and taking extra bases on hits to the field's spacious outfield.

in 1971. Otis was selected to five All-Star Games during the 1970s and won three Gold Glove Awards. The Royals were emphasizing speed and defense. Otis was a big part of this strategy.

Kansas City made other clever trades. The Royals acquired first baseman John Mayberry after the 1971 season from the Houston Astros and outfielder Hal McRae from the Cincinnati Reds following the 1972 season. Both would develop into mainstays in Kansas City's lineup.

The Royals' biggest addition in putting together a championship-caliber club, however, came through MLB's annual amateur draft. In the second round of the 1971 draft, Kansas City chose George Brett. Brett was an 18-year-old who had excelled at El Segundo High School in

Left to right, first baseman John Mayberry, second baseman Cookie Rojas, and center fielder Amos Otis pose at Royals Stadium in the 1970s.

Southern California. His older brother Ken was a pitcher with the Boston Red Sox.

Two years later, Brett made his debut with the Royals. Within just a couple of years, Brett would develop into one of the finest hitters in baseball.

On April 10, 1973, the Royals opened their new baseball-only ballpark, Royals Stadium, with a 12–1 win over the Texas Rangers. The ballpark's most noteworthy features were the waterfalls and fountains that spewed water into the hot Midwestern air behind the outfield fences. The stadium also had a $2.7 million scoreboard.

The Royals hosted the All-Star Game in their first season in their new stadium. Otis and Mayberry were in the AL's starting lineup. The AL lost 7–1 to the NL in front of 40,849. Royals Stadium, the first ballpark in the AL with an entire field that had artificial turf, made an impression on baseball fans watching across the country.

The Royals had more than a stadium to showcase as the 1970s marched on. Right-hander Steve Busby went 22–14 in 1974. Brett quickly became a standout that year at third base. In 1975, he batted .308 with 195 hits, 11 homers, and 89 RBIs. That season, the Royals went a team-best 91–71 and finished in second place in the AL West. Kansas City's new manager in 1975 was Whitey Herzog. He replaced Jack McKeon, who was fired in July of that year.

In 1976, the Royals finally passed Oakland. The Athletics had won the previous five AL West titles. Kansas City finished 90–72, 2 1/2 games ahead of Oakland, to win the division crown. The Royals advanced to the postseason for the first time. Brett hit .333 to win his first AL batting title. He collected 215 hits. He also had 21 steals. He

Al Cowens, *left*, Hal McRae, *middle*, and John Mayberry smile after Kansas City won Game 1 of the 1977 ALCS. But the Yankees would capture that series and frustrate the Royals often in the late 1970s.

was one of seven Royals with 20 stolen bases or more.

Kansas City faced the New York Yankees in the ALCS. It would become a familiar sight. The teams would match up in three straight ALCS series from 1976 to 1978. The Royals fought the mighty Yankees tooth and nail. But New York was simply too good each time. The Yankees

Hal McRae

Outfielder/designated hitter Hal McRae quickly became a fixture for the Royals after the team acquired him from the Cincinnati Reds in November 1972. McRae had a break-out season in 1974, batting .310 with 15 homers and 88 RBIs. McRae would play with the Royals for the rest of his career, until 1987. He batted better than .300 in six full seasons with the team and finished fourth in the AL MVP race in both 1976 and 1982.

won three games to two in both 1976 and 1977, and then three games to one in 1978. New York, which featured stars such as Reggie Jackson during this era, went on to win the World Series in 1977 and 1978.

The Royals had built one of baseball's most talented

rosters. In addition to an excellent offense and defense, the team had strong pitching. Right-hander Dennis Leonard earned 20 and 21 wins in 1977 and 1978, respectively. Paul Splittorff won 15 games or more four times in the 1970s. Fellow left-hander Larry Gura had a breakout season in 1978. He went 16–4.

But the Royals had run into Yankees teams that were just a little bit better. Kansas City was still confident in its future, however. And with Brett's help, including a spectacular season to open the 1980s, the Royals would continue to be contenders well into the next decade.

Whitey Herzog

Whitey Herzog was a big-league outfielder and first baseman from 1956 to 1963 for four teams, including the Kansas City Athletics. He managed the Texas Rangers in 1973 and the California Angels in 1974 before taking the manager's job with the Royals in 1975. He won three AL West titles with Kansas City. But he was let go after a second-place finish in 1979. He then became the St. Louis Cardinals' manager and led them to three World Series, winning the title in 1982. Herzog and the Cardinals lost to the Royals in the 1985 World Series. Herzog was known as the "White Rat" because of his white hair.

Whitey Herzog, shown in 1977, managed the Royals to AL West titles in 1976, 1977, and 1978. In 2010, he made the Baseball Hall of Fame.

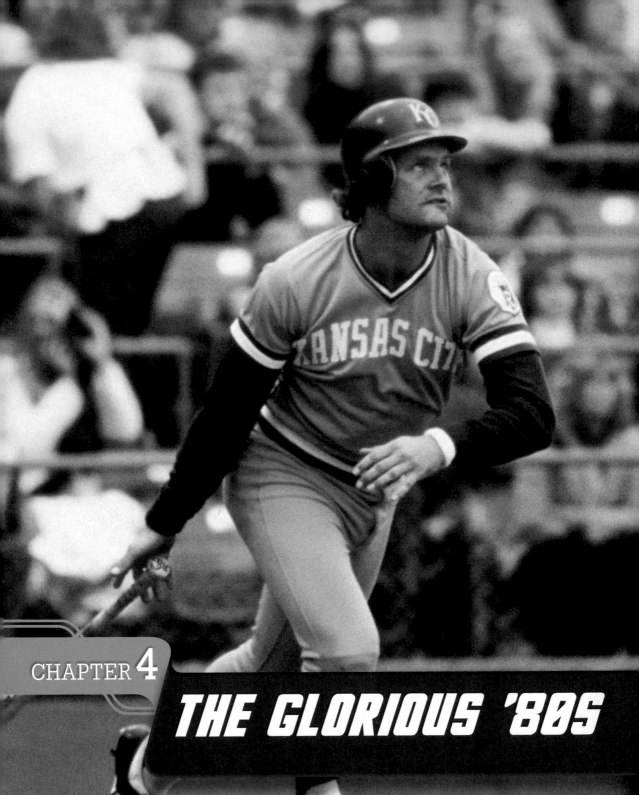

CHAPTER **4**

THE GLORIOUS '80S

By the time the 1980s rolled around, the Royals were ready to reach baseball's biggest stage. They had won three straight AL West titles in the late 1970s, only to fall to the powerful New York Yankees each time in the ALCS. Kansas City wanted to take the next step and make the World Series.

The Royals had almost won a fourth consecutive AL West crown in 1979. Kansas City finished 85–77, three games behind the California Angels. Manager Whitey Herzog was let go after the season. Former Baltimore Orioles hitting and first-base coach Jim Frey was his replacement.

That's Incredible

George Brett's 1980 season was remarkable. Brett hit .390, which through 2013 was the second-best batting average in the past 72 years to the .394 average the San Diego Padres' Tony Gwynn had in a strike-shortened 1994 season. Brett missed 45 games in 1980 because of injuries. He still had 175 hits, 24 of them home runs. He also had 118 RBIs in his 117 games.

Kansas City's George Brett watches a ball he hit during the 1980 regular season. Brett chased a .400 batting average that year but settled for .390.

The Royals enjoyed a special season in 1980. Left fielder Willie Wilson had 79 stolen bases and a major league-best 133 runs and 230 hits. He also won a Gold Glove Award. Pitcher Dennis Leonard finished 20–11. Reliever Dan Quisenberry, in his second season, earned a major league-high 33 saves. Kansas City went 97–65 and easily claimed the AL West title.

Dan Quisenberry

As the relief-pitcher role of closer became more popular in the late 1970s and early 1980s, the Royals developed one of the best. Dan Quisenberry led the AL in saves in 1980 (with 33), 1982 (35), 1983 (45), 1984 (44), and 1985 (37). Quisenberry, a right-hander, threw in a sidearm style and had excellent control. He struggled in 1988 with Kansas City and was released. He retired from the majors in 1990. Tragically, Quisenberry died in 1998 at age 45 after a battle with brain cancer.

But nothing captured the attention of Royals fans, and the baseball world, more than George Brett's chase after a .400 batting average. No big-league player had hit .400 since 1941. That year, the legendary Ted Williams batted .406 for the Boston Red Sox.

After he went 2-for-4 in the Royals' 13–3 victory over the visiting Oakland Athletics on September 19, Brett was at exactly .400. He could not, however, keep up the torrid pace. He ended up with a .390 batting average.

The drama of Kansas City's season had just begun. The Royals faced the Yankees in the ALCS again. Kansas City finally got over the hump, sweeping New York in three games. Brett hit a three-run homer off ace reliever Goose Gossage in the seventh inning of Game 3. Kansas City won

Manager Jim Frey, *middle*, leads his players off the field after the Royals beat the Yankees 3–2 in Game 2 of the 1980 ALCS.

4–2 at Yankee Stadium. For the first time, the Royals earned a spot in the World Series.

The Philadelphia Phillies, however, made sure that the Royals would not celebrate a world title. Philadelphia—led by stars such as third baseman Mike Schmidt, first baseman Pete Rose, and pitcher Steve Carlton—beat Kansas City four games to two.

Kansas City made the playoffs again in 1981. The

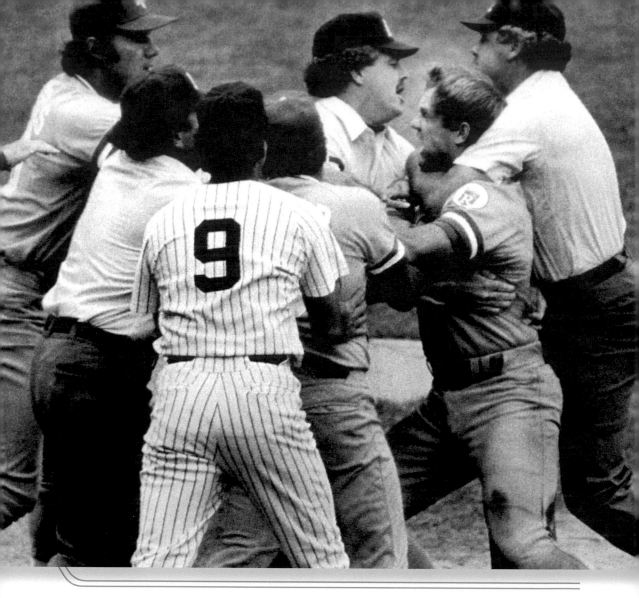

The Royals' George Brett, *right*, has to be held back after he was called out on July 24, 1983, at Yankee Stadium in the "Pine Tar Game."

season was split into halves because of a players' strike. The Royals won the AL West's second-half title with a 30–23 record. Dick Howser, the Yankees' manager in 1980, replaced Frey as the Royals' manager in the second half of the year. Kansas City faced first-half AL West champion

"Pine Tar Game"

George Brett went into a rage on July 24, 1983, at Yankee Stadium. After Brett hit a two-run, ninth-inning home run off the Yankees' Goose Gossage with two outs to give the Royals a 5–4 lead, home-plate umpire Tim McClelland called Brett out to end the game. McClelland had examined Brett's bat and decided that the pine tar on it had exceeded the legal 18 inches. Yankees manager Billy Martin had asked McClelland to look at the bat. It was a little-known rule. Brett sprinted from the Royals' dugout to argue with McClelland and had to be restrained. Kansas City appealed the umpire's decision. AL president Lee MacPhail ruled in the Royals' favor, and on August 18 they finished off a 5–4 suspended-game win in New York.

Oakland in a special division playoff series and lost three games to none. The Royals placed second in the division each of the next two seasons. Kansas City made it back to the postseason in 1984. The Royals won the AL West with an 84–78 record. In the ALCS, the Detroit Tigers swept Kansas City.

All the pieces came together for a world-title season in 1985. At the plate, the Royals were a veteran team. Third baseman Brett, second baseman Frank White, and designated hitter Hal McRae had been with Kansas City for years. But several of the Royals' starting pitchers were young. Bret Saberhagen was the staff ace at age 21. He went 20–6 and won the AL Cy Young Award. Danny Jackson, 23, and Mark Gubicza, 22, both won 14 games.

The Royals won the AL West at 91–71. They then rallied against Toronto in the ALCS and St. Louis in the World Series to win it all. Kansas City celebrated with a downtown parade in which 225,000 fans turned out.

Kansas City remained competitive for the rest of the

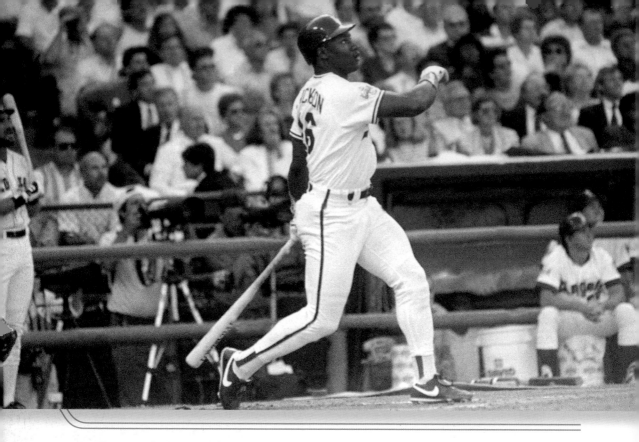

Kansas City's Bo Jackson watches the flight of his mammoth homer in the first inning of the 1989 All-Star Game in Anaheim, California.

Dick Howser

Dick Howser was the Royals' popular manager in 1985, when they won the World Series. The former big-league infielder managed the Yankees in 1980. He led them to a 103–59 record but was fired after New York was swept by Kansas City in the ALCS. A year later, the Royals hired Howser to replace Jim Frey. Howser managed the team until the 1986 season. He became ill and was diagnosed with a brain tumor. On June 17, 1987, he passed away.

1980s. But the Royals could not get back to the playoffs. Kansas City finished in second place at 83–79 in 1987. Rookie Kevin Seitzer became the everyday third baseman. Brett moved over to first base. Seitzer racked up an AL-high 207 hits. Right fielder Danny Tartabull had 34 homers and 101 RBIs. Left fielder Bo Jackson, a remarkable athlete who also played pro football, emerged with 22 homers. Saberhagen finished 18–10.

The Royals went 84–77 in 1988 and placed third in the AL West. Gubicza finished 20–8. It was Kansas City's first full season with John Wathan as manager. He was a former utility player for the team from 1976 to 1985.

Kansas City improved to 92–70 in 1989. The Royals placed second. Saberhagen went 23–6 with a 2.16 ERA to capture his second Cy Young Award. Rookie Tom "Flash" Gordon compiled a 17–9 record.

The 1980s had come to an end. The success that the Royals began enjoying in the 1970s carried over into the next decade. Unfortunately for Kansas City, losing would soon become the norm.

BO JACKSON

In the late 1980s, two-sport star Bo Jackson became a national sensation.

Jackson had been a college football standout at Auburn University in Alabama. He also was a talented baseball player. The Royals drafted the outfielder in 1986. In 1987, he hit 22 homers with Kansas City in just 116 games. Jackson ended up also playing in the NFL with the Los Angeles Raiders, joining them after the Royals' seasons ended.

Jackson—who possessed speed, power, and a strong throwing arm—had his best year for Kansas City in 1989, when he had 32 homers and 105 RBIs. He played in his only All-Star Game that year. He won the MVP Award in the AL's 5–3 victory over the NL in Anaheim, California. He hit a 448-foot homer to lead off the bottom of the first. Jackson played with the Royals through 1990 before finishing his career with the Chicago White Sox and the California Angels.

CHAPTER 5

BEGINNING OF DECLINE

As the 1990s got underway, many of the key members of the Royals' 1985 championship team were no longer with Kansas City. The Royals had enjoyed successful, winning baseball for a long time. But that would change in the new decade.

The retirement of second baseman Frank White after the 1990 season was followed by George Brett playing his final game in 1993. All-time Royals steals leader Willie Wilson left for the Oakland Athletics after the 1990 season via free agency. Bo Jackson's baseball performances suffered after he injured his hip while playing football with the Los Angeles Raiders. Kansas City released him before the 1991 season. Beloved owner Ewing Kauffman died of bone cancer in August 1993. His death came less than one month after Royals Stadium was renamed Kauffman Stadium.

Royals manager Hal McRae argues with umpire Joe Brinkman on September 1, 1993, in Milwaukee. McRae managed the Royals from 1991 to 1994. The team never finished better than third place during that time.

The Royals began to play poorly on the field. They had just three teams with winning records in the 1990s. The 1992 team, managed by former Royals star Hal McRae in his second season in charge, was the first Kansas City squad to lose 90 games since the 1970 team. The Royals finished 72–90.

The hiring of McRae as manager in 1991, to replace John Wathan, did produce a rare father-and-son tandem.

The Royals selected Hal's son Brian in the first round of the 1985 amateur draft. Brian was promoted from the minor leagues to the big-league team in 1990. He then played for his dad in 1991. The center fielder was with the Royals for five years. Hal managed Kansas City until 1994. Ex-Royal Bob Boone replaced McRae after he was fired.

Kansas City had other special moments in the 1990s. Some of them involved Brett. In 1990, he hit .329 to win his third batting title. Brett had also won batting crowns in 1976 and 1980. He became the first player in baseball history to win batting titles in three different decades.

Brett hit .285 in 1992. In the season's final week, on September 30 against the host California Angels, Brett recorded his 3,000th hit. It was

George Brett connects for a single in the Royals' 4–0 win over the host Angels on September 30, 1992. The hit was Brett's 3,000th for his career.

a single during the seventh inning of a 4–0 win for Kansas City. Brett went 4-for-5 in the game. He became the 18th player to reach the 3,000-hit mark in major league history.

The next year was Brett's 20th full season with the Royals. He announced that he would retire after the end of the season. In his final at-bat, in the last game of the year against the host Texas Rangers, Brett lined a single for his 3,154th career hit.

Brett's No. 5 jersey was retired at Kauffman Stadium on April 7, 1997. Brett became a vice president of baseball operations with the Royals after his

ROYALS' KING

You will get little argument that George Brett is the greatest player in Royals history. In fact, many baseball historians rank him among the best third basemen ever. Bill James, one of the most famous of those historians, placed Brett only behind the Philadelphia Phillies' Mike Schmidt, who played during the same era as Brett.

Brett, who was inducted into the Baseball Hall of Fame in 1999, batted .305 over parts of 21 seasons and is the all-time leader in numerous offensive categories for the Royals. He won three batting titles and also led the AL in hits and triples three times. He compiled 3,154 hits during his career.

Brett was a fierce competitor who excelled in the postseason. In 43 career playoff games, he batted .337 with 10 home runs and 23 RBIs.

playing days were over. He also was a part-time coach.

Kansas City's struggles continued on the field as the 1990s went on. After an 84–78 campaign in 1993, the Royals would not win more than 75 games in a season for the rest of the decade. Even the stadium in Kansas City was not quite the same as those glory years. The artificial turf was replaced by natural grass before the 1995 season.

The Royals did have some talented players in the 1990s. Right-hander Kevin Appier finished 18–8 with an AL-best 2.56 ERA in 1993. Mike Sweeney made his debut in 1995 as a catcher. By 1999, he was a first baseman and designated hitter and was putting up big numbers: 22 homers, 102 RBIs, and a .322 batting average. That same year, Kansas City could boast of a

The Royals' Carlos Beltran swings in 1999. Indians catcher Einar Diaz is on the left. Beltran had 22 homers and 108 RBIs as a rookie that season.

talented trio of young outfielders—Johnny Damon in left, AL Rookie of the Year Carlos Beltran in center, and Jermaine Dye in right. Beltran and Dye both had more than 20 homers and 100 RBIs. Damon hit .307 and scored 101 runs.

Kansas City's pitchers struggled mightily in 1999, however. As a result, the Royals finished just 64–97. That put them in last place in the AL Central. They had joined the division in 1994. The AL and the NL reorganized into leagues with three divisions each that year.

Kansas City had fared poorly for most of the 1990s. Things would only get worse in the 2000s.

CHAPTER 6

STRIVING FOR A COMEBACK

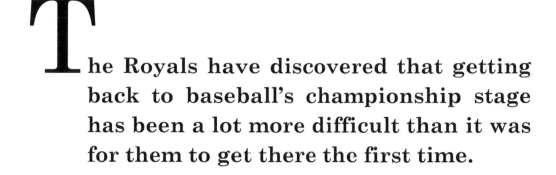

The Royals have discovered that getting back to baseball's championship stage has been a lot more difficult than it was for them to get there the first time.

In 2000, the Glass family became the first permanent owners of the Royals since Ewing Kauffman died in 1993. But the new owners could not change Kansas City's fortunes.

Every season in the 2000s was a losing year for Kansas City, except for 2003. The Royals lost 100 games or more in 2002, 2004, 2005, and 2006. Former major league catcher Tony Pena managed the team to first place for much of the 2003 season. But Kansas City finished in third at 83–79.

It was not that the Royals did not have talented players. It was that they did not have enough of them, or that the small-market team could not afford to hang on to its stars.

Each season in 1999, 2001, 2002, and 2003, switch-hitting

Mike Sweeney watches a ball he hit in 2004. Sweeney continued his standout play, but the Royals finished an AL-worst 58–104 that season.

center fielder Carlos Beltran had at least 22 homers, 100 RBIs, and 27 stolen bases. But Kansas City decided that it could not afford to keep him. The Royals dealt him to the Houston Astros as part of a three-team trade in 2004. Kansas City received third baseman/outfielder Mark Teahen and pitcher Mike Wood from the Oakland Athletics and catcher John Buck from the Astros. Teahen and Buck became regular contributors. But Wood struggled.

Standout first baseman/designated hitter Mike Sweeney did stay with the Royals for many years. He made his debut with the team in 1995. In 2000, he batted .333 with 29 homers and a club-record 144 RBIs. Sweeney hit for power and average for several more seasons before injuries slowed him down. Kansas City allowed him to sign with Oakland after the 2007 season.

Two pitchers provided the biggest highlights for the Royals in the second half of the decade. Kansas City signed Joakim Soria after the San Diego Padres left him available. The right-hander had 42 saves in 2008 and continued to thrive as the closer the next two seasons.

The starting staff also had a future star in right-hander Zack Greinke. Greinke

Zack Greinke

Kansas City chose right-hander Zack Greinke in the first round, sixth overall, in the 2002 amateur draft. The Florida native had a strong rookie season in 2004, but he struggled the next few years. He battled depression and social anxiety disorder and missed significant time. He returned to the rotation in 2008 and went 13–10. He then enjoyed a remarkable 2009 season in which he won the AL Cy Young Award despite playing for a 65–97 team. Greinke had 242 strikeouts.

Zack Greinke prepares to deliver a pitch in 2009. Greinke began his Cy Young Award-winning season by throwing 24 straight scoreless innings.

had finished 8–11 in 2004 and placed fourth in the AL Rookie of the Year voting. He struggled during the next several seasons but enjoyed a brilliant year in 2009. Greinke was 16–8 with a major league-best 2.16 ERA and won the AL Cy Young Award.

Billy Butler also emerged as a talented player. In 2012, he hit .313, had 29 home runs, and earned a Silver Slugger.

In 2013, the Royals saw their first winning season since 2003, finishing 86–76. That record wasn't enough for the playoffs. Still, left fielder Alex Gordon took home his third consecutive Gold Glove. And, the season gave Kansas City's fans hope that the Royals could someday return to the winning ways that were common for them in the 1970s and 1980s.

TIMELINE

1968 — Ewing Kauffman is granted an MLB franchise for Kansas City. The team, named the Royals, would begin play in the AL in the 1969 season.

1973 — After four seasons at Municipal Stadium, Kansas City opens its new ballpark, Royals Stadium, with a 12–1 win over the Texas Rangers on April 10.

1976 — The Royals capture their first AL West championship, finishing 90–72. The New York Yankees defeat Kansas City three games to two in the ALCS.

1977 — Kansas City goes a team-best 102–60 to win the AL West again. The Royals, however, lose to the Yankees in five games in the ALCS for a second consecutive year.

1978 — The Royals win a third straight AL West crown under manager Whitey Herzog. They again face the Yankees in the ALCS and again lose, this time three games to one.

1980 — The Royals' George Brett flirts with becoming the first big-league player to hit .400 since 1941. Brett finishes at .390 and is chosen the AL's MVP. Kansas City goes 97–65 under first-year manager Jim Frey and wins the AL West. The Royals finally top the Yankees in the ALCS, sweeping them in three games. In its first World Series, Kansas City falls four games to two to the Philadelphia Phillies.

1985 — The Royals compile a 91–71 record to claim the AL West title again. Bret Saberhagen finishes 20–6 and wins the AL Cy Young Award. Kansas City overcomes three-games-to-one deficits to beat the Toronto Blue Jays in the ALCS and the St. Louis Cardinals in the World Series. Saberhagen's five-hitter helps the host Royals win 11–0 in Game 7 of the Series on October 27.

1987	Dick Howser, who managed the Royals to the 1985 World Series championship, dies of cancer on June 17. Kansas City retires his No. 10 uniform the next month.
1989	Saberhagen wins his second Cy Young Award after going 23–6 to lead the AL in wins and also compiling a league-best 2.16 ERA.
1992	Brett reaches the 3,000-hit mark, becoming the 18th player in big-league history to do so, with a seventh-inning single in the Royals' 4–0 win over the host California Angels on September 30. Brett finishes the game 4-for-5, with his fourth hit being the key 3,000th.
1993	Brett plays his last major league game, hitting a single in his final at-bat in the Royals' 4–1 victory over the host Rangers in the regular-season finale on October 3. Brett finishes with 3,154 career hits.
2003	The Royals win their first nine games overall and their first 11 at home. Kansas City leads the AL Central by 7 1/2 games at one point and is tied for the division lead in late August. But the Royals falter down the stretch and finish in third place at 83–79.
2005	Kansas City finishes a team-worst 56–106, losing the most games in the major leagues that year. The season is part of a five-year stretch in which the Royals lose 100 or more games four times.
2009	Despite playing for a last-place team, Kansas City ace right-hander Zack Greinke finishes 16–8 with a major league-best 2.16 ERA and wins the AL Cy Young Award.
2013	Left fielder Alex Gordon earns his third consecutive Gold Glove as the Royals post their first winning season since 2003.

QUICK STATS

FRANCHISE HISTORY
1969–

WORLD SERIES
(wins in bold)
1980, **1985**

AL CHAMPIONSHIP SERIES
1976, 1977, 1978, 1980, 1984, 1985

DIVISION CHAMPIONSHIPS
1976, 1977, 1978, 1980,
1981 (second half), 1984, 1985

KEY PLAYERS
(position[s]; seasons with team)
Kevin Appier (SP; 1989–99, 2003–04)
Carlos Beltran (CF; 1998–2004)
George Brett (3B/1B/DH; 1973–93)
Zack Greinke (SP; 2004–10)
Mark Gubicza (SP; 1984–96)

Bo Jackson (OF; 1986–90)
Dennis Leonard (SP; 1974–83,
    1985–86)
John Mayberry (1B; 1972–77)
Hal McRae (DH/OF; 1973–87)
Amos Otis (CF; 1970–83)
Freddie Patek (SS; 1971–79)
Lou Piniella (LF; 1969–73)
Dan Quisenberry (RP; 1979–88)
Bret Saberhagen (SP; 1984–91)
Paul Splittorff (SP; 1970–84)
Mike Sweeney (DH/1B/C;
    1995–2007)
Frank White (2B; 1973–90)
Willie Wilson (OF; 1976–90)

KEY MANAGERS
Jim Frey (1980–81):
    127–105; 5–4 (postseason)
Whitey Herzog (1975–79):
    410–304; 5-9 (postseason)
Dick Howser (1981–86):
    404–365; 8-12 (postseason)

HOME PARKS
Municipal Stadium (1969–72)
Kauffman Stadium (1973–)
    Known as Royals Stadium
    (1973–93)

* All statistics through 2013 season

QUOTES AND ANECDOTES

Harmon Killebrew played with the Minnesota Twins for most of his 22-year Hall of Fame career. Killebrew, however, spent his final big-league season with Kansas City in 1975. Killebrew played in 106 games, mostly as a designated hitter, and had 14 home runs. He hit the final homer of his career, number 573, on September 18 in the Royals' 4–3 road victory over, ironically, the Twins. When he retired, Killebrew ranked fifth on baseball's all-time home-run list.

"The game beat me. It beats everybody. It took 26 years to beat Nolan Ryan, but it did. Now it's beaten me."
—Royals star George Brett, after he retired following the 1993 season

George Brett was named to the AL All-Star team 13 times during his career, giving him by far the most invitations to the Midsummer Classic in Royals history. Through 2013, the Kansas City players with the next most All-Star Game invites were Amos Otis, Mike Sweeney, and Frank White, all of whom had five.

On September 7, 1971, in the Royals' 4–3 victory over the visiting Milwaukee Brewers, Amos Otis stole five bases. It was the first time in 44 years that a big-league base runner had achieved this feat.

"I want to thank all the pitchers who couldn't go nine innings, and manager Dick Howser, who wouldn't let them."
—Kansas City closer Dan Quisenberry, after he compiled an AL-best 35 saves in 1982 and was named the league's Fireman of the Year by the *Sporting News*

GLOSSARY

ace

A team's best starting pitcher.

acquire

To add a player, usually through the draft, free agency, or a trade.

berth

A place, spot, or position, such as in the baseball playoffs.

closer

A relief pitcher who is called on to pitch, usually in the ninth inning, to protect his team's lead.

expansion

In sports, the addition of a franchise or franchises to a league.

franchise

An entire sports organization, including the players, coaches, and staff.

market

The city in which a team plays.

postseason

The games in which the best teams play after the regular-season schedule has been completed.

retire

To officially end one's career.

rookie

A first-year player in the major leagues.

roster

The players as a whole on a baseball team.

switch-hitter

A batter who can hit left-handed or right-handed.

veteran

An individual with great experience in a particular endeavor.

FOR MORE INFORMATION

Further Reading

Kansas City Star. *George Brett: A Royal Hero.* Champaign, IL: Sports Publishing LLC, 2001.

Spivak, Jeffrey. *Crowning the Kansas City Royals: Remembering the 1985 World Series Champs.* Champaign, IL: Sports Publishing LLC, 2005.

Vecsey, George. *Baseball: A History of America's Favorite Game.* New York: Modern Library, 2008.

Websites

To learn more about Inside MLB, visit **booklinks.abdopublishing.com**. These links are routinely monitored and updated to provide the most current information available.

Places to Visit

Kauffman Stadium
One Royal Way
Kansas City, MO 64129
1-800-6ROYALS
royals.mlb.com/kc/ballpark/
This has been the Royals' home field since 1973. The team plays 81 regular-season games here each year. Tours are available when the Royals are not playing.

National Baseball Hall of Fame and Museum
25 Main Street
Cooperstown, NY 13326
1-888-HALL-OF-FAME
www.baseballhall.org
This hall of fame and museum highlights the greatest players and moments in the history of baseball. Former Royals star George Brett is enshrined here.

Surprise Stadium
15850 North Bullard Avenue
Surprise, AZ 85374
623-222-2222
www.surpriseaz.gov/files/springtraining
This has been the Royals' spring-training ballpark since 2003. It also serves as the spring home of the Texas Rangers.

INDEX

About the Author

Paul Bowker is a freelance writer and author based in Ponte Vedra, Florida. He was a resident of Kansas City, Missouri, when the Royals won the World Series in 1985. His 25-year newspaper career includes a stint as a sports copy editor at the *Kansas City Star*, and he has covered four World Series. He has won many national, regional, and state awards as a writer and an editor, and he is a past president of the Associated Press Sports Editors. He lives with his wife and daughter.